The Prestige S
The Thirtie

John Banks
Photography by G H F Atkins

**With additional material from the Senior Transport Archive
and the Cull Collection**

Front cover: In the 1930s the small bus with around 25 seats achieved perhaps its most sophisticated form in the Dennis Mace, which had the driver alongside the engine in true forward-control configuration. Southern National's No. **668** (**BTA 59**) is a 1935 example with Eastern Counties 26-seat bodywork. *(John Banks)*

Title page: G J Rackham, Chief Engineer at AEC from 1st October 1928 after a brief spell with Leyland Motors in a similar post, designed a new range of chassis, including a two-axled double-decker, the Regent. The new model made a big impact in many fleets, especially municipalities, in the 1930s, not to mention the thousands that ran for London Transport. Birmingham's No. **479** (**OV 4479**) was a 1931 example with Short Bros highbridge 48-seat bodywork, which was withdrawn in 1944. Its chassis was then used as the basis for a Birmingham Corporation service vehicle; as such it lasted until 1959. *(GHFA)*

Below: As the 1930s dawned the seaside tripper's transport was often still the canvas-roofed charabanc, a design which had reached the pinnacle of its development in the mid 1920s. These two examples, **HW 1634**, an Associated Daimler, and an unidentified make **YC 2192**, were parked close to the beach under the cliffs at a West Country resort. *(GHFA)*

>> *Opposite page:* A special vehicle for a special job. Number **1** in the West Mon. fleet was a Leyland Bull TSQ1 goods chassis registered **WO 4625**, bought in 1930 for use on the notorious Bargoed Hill route, for which the chassis was fitted with sprag brakes to prevent run-back. The body was a 34-seat dual-doorway unit by Christopher Dodson, of Willesden. The vehicle was withdrawn, after a hard life, in 1949, though the body was reused on a Foden, HWO 590. *(STA/BCVM)*

Inside back cover and back cover: The London scene of the 1930s is recalled in these views of **T31** (**UU 6646**), an early member of the T class of AEC Regals; **Q83** (**CGJ 188**), an example of the revolutionary side-engined AEC Q type; and **RT113** (**FXT 288**). The latter entered service early in 1940, but the London Transport Chiswick-designed RT was a true child of the 1930s, intended to replace the STL. *(All: John Banks)*

INTRODUCTION

It is probably safe to say that there are no public service vehicles which were on the roads in the 1930s still running today outside the loving hands of the preservation movement. Fortunately for us the art of photography was no longer in its infancy as the twenties gave way to the thirties. Decades of searching have led to the reluctant acceptance that some 1930s buses and coaches were never photographed, either officially or by amateurs, but enough were to allow us a good idea of how the public transport scene appeared between 70 and 80 years ago.

A prominent contributor to this happy state of affairs is the Nottingham-based photographer G H F Atkins, a friend of the writer for approaching 40 years. Geoffrey took his first bus picture in 1927 in the seaside resort of Skegness. He had been given a modest camera at the age of 15 as a reward for scholastic endeavour and was thus able to set about providing himself with a collection of illustrations for his great interest, which was - and remains - the art of the coachbuilder.

Despite the restrictions of a youthful lack of cash and never having owned a motor vehicle, Geoffrey Atkins went on from that modest start to build up a set of equipment and a technique -

both behind the camera and in the darkroom - second to none. Some of his collection's greatest glories stem from the 1930s, which happened to be a decade of outstanding interest in bus and coach development. Thus when this volume on that decade was mooted, writer and publisher were off to a flying start when Geoffrey once again courteously and willingly made his work available.

But why was that decade different? What makes its vehicles so attractive through our backward-looking spectacles? Sheer variety is a good place to start. As the 1920s gave way to the 1930s an operator might have chosen among perhaps threescore chassis manufacturers, a goodly proportion of them based overseas, and as many, if not more, coachbuilders.

Some of them are virtually forgotten these days: Albion, Gilford, Maudslay, Morris, W&G du Cros and many another are nostalgic names; others such as AEC, Bedford, Bristol, Daimler, Guy - even Leyland - made more impact on the market and survived rather longer but eventually succumbed to unfortunate commercial management decisions. Dennis, one of the earlier companies in the field, has come into the new Millennium as a major chassis supplier and is one of the few direct links between that far-off time and our own.

MAINTENANCE INSTRUCTIONS

FOR THE

"Bristol"

LOW-LOADING

LIGHT PASSENGER CHASSIS.

(TYPE "B")

MANUFACTURED BY

THE BRISTOL TRAMWAYS & CARRIAGE CO., LTD.

Codes:
A B C 5TH EDITION,

OFFICES AND WORKS:

Telegrams:
"AUTOMOBILE, BRISTOL."

MARCONI.

BRISTOL, ENGLAND.

Telephone:
BRISTOL 20001

A novel way of gaining an appreciation of the 1930s bus industry granted the writer recently was the discovery in the local bric-à-brac shop of a cache of handbooks and manuals relating to some of the era's buses and trolleybuses, which had clearly belonged to someone who had held an engineering position within the industry, perhaps with Manchester Corporation.

The gem among them was undoubtedly a copy in fine condition of the "Maintenance Instructions for the Bristol Low-Loading Light Passenger Chassis (Type B)". Its title page and a drawing of a B-type chassis are reproduced and the over-riding impression gained is just how simple the Bristol B was. Today's high-tech integrally constructed machines with their complicated electronics, fail-safe devices (that often put a bus out of service because of a sticking switch), sophisticated engines, suspensions and transmissions, are so far an advance over the rugged simplicity of the early Bristol that one is lost for the means to compare them.

An interesting little book entitled "The Modern Diesel" (undated but apparently published about 1936) from the same source gives a set of figures to prove that an oil-engined bus running at 12 tons gross weight would use less than half the fuel of its petrol-engined counterpart. It also made the interesting statement that Gardner engines were outstandingly easy to start by hand. As a former owner of a 1942 Bristol K5G (who can still feel the bruises after 30 years), the writer begs to differ.

The next item in this little treasure trove is a service manual for Leyland trolleybuses, which relates to only 10 vehicles, of type TB6, chassis numbers 13611-20. The writer, whose mechanical ability is confined to topping up water in the radiator and - if absolutely necessary - changing sparking plugs, was often baffled in his youthful enthusiasm as to exactly what was going on in the bowels of the machinery to accompany certain of the driver's actions. That ratchet handbrake, for example: here it is, fully explained and - again - so simple.

Physics lessons at school had imparted a hazy knowledge of how the reciprocating motion of an internal combustion engine was converted through a transmission system to turn the back (usually, in those days) wheels of a motor vehicle, but to a certain grubby, ink-covered schoolboy, how a trolleybus worked was another mystery.

The bric-à-brac shop discovery has solved

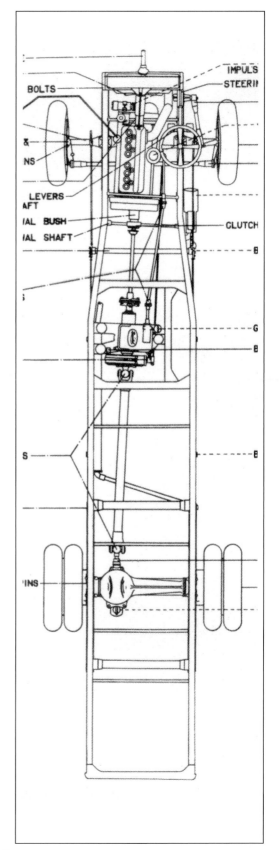

Above: How did it work? What was the trolleybus driver doing with all that frantic pulling on the handbrake lever? The mystery is solved through this illustration of the beautifully simple engineering of the Leyland TB6 ratchet handbrake mechanism.

Below: One of several illustrations from the Metropolitan-Vickers brochure that explain the workings of a trolleybus. This one is a Karrier fitted - as might be expected - with Metropolitan-Vickers's own electrical equipment. (Both: John Banks Collection)

that one, too, through a 1937 booklet - "Trolleybus Electrical Equipment" - put out by the Metropolitan-Vickers Electrical Company Limited, which explains - with the aid of copious photographs, drawings and graphs - everything from regenerative control systems to radio interference suppression coils and leakage testing sockets.

Items on Gardner engines and Kirkstall axles complete this little treasure trove and what a pity one could not have had such reading in more youthful times. It would have been of more use than "Treasure Island".

Although by 1930 "traditional" buses had achieved a configuration that was to be the norm for the next 30 years (front-engines, usually rear-entrances, open platforms but enclosed staircases), the 1930s was nevertheless a decade of development. Just how much so is reinforced by a browse through the pages of the trade press. "Bus & Coach", for example, in 1934, had numerous learned authors dealing with a variety of more or less controversial matters.

"The State Scores when Buses replace Trams" intoned the charismatic R Stuart Pilcher, FRSE, M Inst T, General Manager of Manchester Corporation Transport Department, whilst his colleague T G Richardson, M Inst T, Engineer and General Manager of the Rhondda Tramways Company Limited went one further and actually told the industry "How to change over from Trams to Buses". Perhaps by then they were preaching to the converted: one way of looking at the electric tramcar industry in the British Isles could conclude that the boom year was somewhere around 1904, after which things went steadily downhill, not least through a

lamentable failure to reinvest in the infrastructure.

G W Hayter, Chief Engineer of the Northern General Transport Company Limited opined that "The Best Position for the Engine is at the Side". He practised what he preached by building side-engined buses for Northern, but history has not agreed with him, despite Rackham's valiant effort with the AEC Q type. Mr Hayter also suggested, however, ideas for locating the engine at the rear, and here he was on safer ground as a fortune-teller.

Very much a thirties preoccupation was an article by P M A Thomas on streamlining bodywork. He commented on various such applications that gave a pleasing "streamlined" appearance but which, in fact, paid little or no attention to the question of wind resistance. In other words, streamlining for purely visual effect is not streamlining.

Articles on "Servicing Diesel Engines", on "Trolleybus Chassis Design" and on "The Trolleybus Simply Explained" were signs of the times, as was one on metal construction of bus bodywork, which looked at the work of pioneer metal body designer Max Meltz at Strachan's

Streamling or mere visual enhancement? The embellishment of Manchester Corporation's Crossley No. 729 (EVR 736) certainly would not have done much to decrease wind resistance. (STA/BCVM)

Wales Farm Road Works. The trolleybus in practical form already had a history (some batches of vehicles had been withdrawn by then), but diesel engines (or compression ignition engines as they were perhaps more accurately termed) and metal-framed bus bodies were exciting new developments in 1934.

Highly germane to that period was a piece entitled "Buying out the Smaller Operator", whose author modestly hid himself behind the pen-name "Speculator". The mopping up of small indepenendents by the major companies was endemic in the thirties: sometimes the means employed to bring the small men to the point where they felt the best thing to do was to cease the struggle and sell out were less than gentlemanly; possibly the use of a pseudonym was a wise precaution.

A fascinating examination of "Why do British and American Bus Designs vary so Greatly" came from the pen of no less a personage that Ernest Boyd Hutchinson, who had in 1912 founded United Automobile Services Limited. He had first-hand knowledge of his subject, having visited the United States in the twenties and ordered some buses from the manufacturer White. Mr Hutchinson had not survived the passage of his company into railway ownership in 1929 and even five years on might have looked at its progress and wished he were still at the helm.

A feature of those issues of Bus & Coach three quarters of a century ago was the series of "Critical Reviews" of contemporary chassis. Those reviewed included, among the small vehicles then available, the Guy Wolf and the Dennis Ace: both 20-seaters; full-sized single-deck chassis included the Gilford Hera and the Sunbeam SF 4/2; the new fashion for diesel-engines manifested itself in reviews of the Crossley Mancunian and Thornycroft Daring double-deckers so equipped.

A period of consolidation hand-in-hand with forward thinking, then, which this book sets out to celebrate in text and pictures.

The invaluable contribution of Geoffrey Atkins (GHFA) has already been mentioned. Geoffrey's material has been augmented by choice items from the Senior Transport Archive (STA) and the Cull Collection (OSMB/CC), the latter now in the safekeeping of the Omnibus Society's Midland Branch. Thanks are again due to the British Commercial Vehicle Museum (BCVM) for generously allowing reproduction of Senior Transport Archive material originating from the old Leyland Motors Limited, and to

Repressive legislation and reactionary, hidebound attitudes to change in the United Kingdom might have been the principal reason why British bus design differed so much from the American. It would not have been legal for a British operator to run this 1938 100-seat trailer bus (above) of American design. The Vancouver Island Coach Lines airsprung Hayes/Leyland of 1936, however, which had luxurious accomodation for only about 25, would seem to have been disqualified only by virtue of its length. (Both: STA/BCVM)

Arnold Richardson for drawing the writer's attention to the Cull Collection and for providing prints.

The writer has as usual shamelessly pestered friends and fellow enthusiasts Ron Maybray and Alan Townsin for confirmation from their comprehensive records of early vehicle details; John Senior has checked the text and made a number of much-appreciated suggestions for its improvement; Philip Battersby and John D Watson have, over the years, been ever generous with their time and knowledge; Keith Healey has kindly loaned contemporary documents and publications held by the Manchester Museum of Transport; the PSV Circle and The Omnibus Society have issued many publications that are invaluable sources of reference to any author seeking to examine British public service vehicles from the enthusiast's standpoint and the debt owed those bodies is once more acknowledged with gratitude; David and Mary Shaw have again read the proofs and corrected those typographical errors that a writer never spots when seeing what he expects to see in his own work.

If despite all their efforts, this work contains inaccuracies, the responsibility is mine alone.

John Banks
Romiley, Cheshire
August 2001

Thirties Independence

A feature of the road traffic scene in the 1930s was the immense variety of PSV chassis makes to be seen in everyday use. This page illustrates one of the less common - even then - and one of the most popular. By 1933 the Sandbach, Cheshire, maker Foden was well-established as a provider of goods-vehicle chassis, but had not managed to make much of an impression on the bus market. **AMB 834** *(above)* was a 1936 DDG6 demonstrator with 48-seat bodywork by Burlingham. It was eventually bought by the Ebor Bus Company, of Mansfield. Leyland, on the other hand, could scarcely keep pace with its order book. This 1938 Roe-bodied Gearless Tiger TS8c, **HL 7110** *(right)*, was No. **420** in the West Riding fleet. *(Both: GHFA)*

<< *Opposite page:* A majestic, stately vehicle in the shape of Thornycroft's 1929 Commercial Motor Show exhibit. **VC 9601** was an FC Forward model, with luxuriously equipped 32-seat coachwork by Strachans. It was sold in 1931 to Tysoe's (Coventry Transport) Limited. In this 1936 view it is in the livery of BTS, also of Coventry, and possibly a successor to Tysoe's.

Above: **TV 2501**, a Renault S1 coach new in 1930 to Bateman and Fines, of Bulwell, reveals the "coal-scuttle" bonnet outline so characteristic of these chassis which had the radiator behind the engine. The coachbuilder is unknown, but could well have been French, with the complete vehicle being exported to England. It was at the north bus park in Skegness during its first summer in service.

Below: An equally rare vehicle was **JC 1121**, a Sunbeam operated by Red Garages, of Llandudno, seen in that town in June 1933. *(All: GHFA)*

<< *Opposite page:* T Burrows & Sons, of Wombwell, had provided **YG 6513**, a 1934 Strachan-bodied Gilford Hera, for a private hire to Scarborough in June 1935. In May 1934, "Bus & Coach" published a critical review of the Hera chassis, which referred in complimentary terms to its silent running, simplicity for maintenance, efficient braking, light steering, clean design and absence of gadgets and concluded that the chassis had many features in advance of others in its class.

Above: Also at the seaside on private hire, this time at Skegness, was **VO 652**, a 1929 Gilford 1660T, bodied by Wycombe Motor Bodies. The vehicle was in the fleet of Waite & Bilby, of Ruddington, who traded as Ideal Coachways.

Below: Another Ruddington-based operator, H Squires & Sons, ran **VO 4408**, a 1930 Rainforth-bodied GMC 20-seater, seen here in Ruddington Market Place in 1936. Later that year the Squires business was acquired by Barton Transport; VO 4408 became Barton No. 246 but was withdrawn immediately and sold to Meadows, of Burton Latimer; thence, via another takeover, it passed to United Counties as fleet number 545 *(All: GHFA)*

<< *Opposite page:* **CT 9025** was a W&G du Cros in the fleet of T A Smith, of Bourne. The rather austere body was by Hall Lewis, whose works were not far from those of W&G du Cros at Acton in north-west London. This picture was taken at the Lawn coach park, Skegness, in July 1930.

Above: In 1930 the Bristol chassis was by no means common. To see an independent's bus-seated version at Scarborough on private hire was perhaps even less so. West Riding's No. **306 (HL 4549)**, a Bristol-bodied 30-seater, new in January 1930 and withdrawn in 1937, was photographed in June 1930.

Below: Keeping the GMC *(see page 13)* company in the Squires of Ruddington fleet was this Crossley with 32-seat Willowbrook bodywork. New in 1931, it passed to Barton as fleet number 243 in 1936 and was withdrawn in 1937. In this view dating from 1935, it was at its base in Ruddington. *(All: GHFA)*

<< *Opposite page:* Yet another Ruddington-based operator was E W Campion, whose fleet included **TV 5630**, a Commer Avenger of purposeful appearance. The Willowbrook body had seating for 32. Campion's business also passed to Barton and this vehicle became Barton's No. 251. It ended its career, via the independent Chappell, of Waddington, in the Lincolnshire Road Car fleet. It was at Ruddington in October 1933.

Above: Campion also had **TV 4021**, another Commer. This one was a Centaur with 20-seat bodywork, again by Willowbrook. This is another October 1933 Ruddington scene. TV 4021 became Barton's No. 249. *(All: GHFA)*

Below: **JL 979**, another Commer Centaur, was new in 1933 and bodied by Brush as a dual-purpose 20-seater. It was owned by W G Turner, of Crowland, who traded as Silver Dawn. It was at Skegness in July 1936.

<< *Opposite page:* Worthington Motor Tours Limited, of Stafford, ran Maudslay ML4 **DRF 207** as fleet number **7**. It is seen in Nottingham in July 1936 when about three months old. The coachbuilder is not known, but is believed to have been based in Coventry. The bonneted layout combined with folding canvas roof was perhaps a conservative specification for 1936, but was in keeping with this operator's traditional ideas.

Above: Outside the Black Boy Hotel in Nottingham's Long Row in August 1935 stands Skill's, of Nottingham, TSM B39B6 No. **14** (**TV 8937**), which had a Strachans coach body and had been new in 1933. It was withdrawn in 1939.

Below: **CHN 995** and **DHN 102** were Nos **49/50** in the fleet of Darlington Triumph Services Limited. They were TSM HA39A7s, dating from 1937, fitted with 35-seat bus bodywork by Northern Coachbuilders. In this June 1937 scene they had when brand new ventured as far as Scarborough on private hire work. Both buses passed to Durham District Services Limited in November 1950. *(All: GHFA)*

Above: A fashionably hatted lady inspects No. **30** (**KD 9406**) of the Merseyside Touring Company at Huntingdon Street, Nottingham, in May 1930. It was working the Liverpool to Great Yarmouth service. The chassis was a TSM B10A and the coachwork, seating 26, was by Burlingham. The vehicle had been new two months earlier, in May 1930; it passed to Ribble as fleet number 1269 in September 1931, with whom it lasted until 1936. It then ran for various small operators until 1939.

Below: This Bristol B, registered **HW 9506**, is recorded as entering service with Bristol Greyhound in 1930. The 26-seat dual-doorway body was by Northern Counties. In this June 1931 view the vehicle was climbing out of Ilfracombe on the joint (with the Merseyside Touring Company) Ilfracombe to Liverpool express service. *(Both: GHFA)*

Dutton's Unity Services, of Nottingham and Sutton-in-Ashfield, had a characterful and varied 16-strong fleet, which was swallowed up by the Trent Motor Traction Company in 1935. Three GMCs, six TSMs, three AEC Regals and four Dennis Lancets were involved. **TV 7472** *(above)* was a 1932 TSM B39A7 with Willowbrook 32-seat bodywork, and **TV 8971** *(below)* was a 1934 AEC Regal 4, bodied by Brush, also as a 32-seater. This pair became Trent's fleet numbers 1217 and 1215. Both were later sold to independent operators (Hulley, of Baslow, and Safeguard, of Guildford) and survived into the postwar era. The photographs on this page were taken outside Dutton's Kent Street, Nottingham, premises, in August 1935 and May 1934. *(Both: GHFA)*

<< *Opposite page:* The Dennis Lancet chassis seems to have been preferred for coaching work by Dutton's and at the time of the takeover by Trent made up a quarter of the fleet. **ATV 4**, a 1935 delivery with Willowbrook 35-seat coachwork, is seen when brand new outside the Kent Street garage. It was numbered 1212 by Trent.

Above: Contemporary with ATV 4 was **ATV 746**, also bodied as a 35-seat coach by Willowbrook. Perhaps it was more of a dual-purpose vehicle: the body is clearly based on Willowbrook's service bus shell and the seats are less luxurious than those in ATV 4. In Trent ownership it assumed the fleet number 1210.

Below: **JU 3060** was a 1931 Dennis Lancet in the fleet of R E Horspool, of Loughborough. Not surprisingly, it was bodied by local coachbuilder Willowbrook, as a 32-seater. Horspool also sold out to Trent, and this vehicle became Trent's No. 1235. It later ran for the independent South Notts, of Gotham. *(All: GHFA)*

<< *Opposite page:* In another picture at the Lawn coach park, Skegness, Geoffrey Atkins has illustrated a popular chassis style - the bonneted 20-seater - of the period. This one, **DO 7533**, was a 1928 Thornycroft A6 operated by Yallop, of Long Sutton, which tipped the scales unladen at 3tons 18cwts 2qtrs.

Above: Photographed in Wells, this is an ADC 424 with Duple 26-seat coachwork. New in July 1928, Bournemouth-registered **RU 6728** was in the Elliott Bros (Royal Blue) fleet. It passed to Hants & Dorset in January 1935 when Elliott was taken over; this coach and others like it were immediately sold. The Dennis alongside was **EL 4814**: another Bournemouth registration.

Below: Another 1928 ADC 424, this time with Hall Lewis 32-seat coachwork. **KH 7091** was in the fleet of D W Burn, of Kingston-upon-Hull, who traded as Grey-de-Luxe. It was photographed on private hire work at Scarborough in June 1935. Note the fixed front and rear sections of the roof with easily detachable canvas centre section; also the then very popular dual-door layout. *(All: GHFA)*

The B & S Motor Service (or Coaches) was the trading name of J Bullock and Sons (1928) Ltd, of Featherstone and Wakefield. Pride of the fleet in the summer of 1934 was No. **161** (**HL 6268**), a Weymann-bodied AEC Q-type 39-seater *(<< opposite page)*. New in June of that year, it lasted until 1943 when it was sold to a dealer and scrapped. The photograph was taken at Huntingdon Street bus station, Nottingham. A 1930 delivery into the B & S fleet *(above)* was No. **113** (**HL 4743**), a Daimler CF6 with 30-seat coachwork by John Taylor Limited, of Barnsley. A close contemporary of the AEC Q was B & S No. **158** (**HL 6095**) *(below)*, a Daimler CP6 new in March 1934, which had 32-seat bus bodywork by Charles Roberts, of Wakefield. The CF6 was withdrawn as early as 1936 but the CP6 soldiered on until 1947. The Daimlers were photographed in exactly the same spot on Scarborough's Marine Drive, but five years apart, in June 1930 and June 1935. *(All: GHFA)*

AECs were prominent on the roads in the 1930s, as they were to be in each succeeding decade until the demise of the marque at the hands of Leyland in the 1960s. The side-engined Q-type was revolutionary, but failed to sell in sufficient numbers to be counted a success. A contemporary of the Bullock example *(page 26)* was No. **16 (AAU 946)** *(above)* in the Skill's, of Nottingham, fleet. Fitted with a Duple body, it had 37 seats, all of which faced forward in this high-floorline design. Skill's took delivery of AAU 946 in May 1934 but clearly did not regard the vehicle very highly, for they sold it in October 1936. It was at the Nottingham Palais. Campion, of Ruddington, some of whose single-deckers we have already seen, had a 1930 AEC Regent with Ransomes 48-seat highbridge bodywork built to the style of the London General's ST type. **JF 223** became Barton Transport No. 248 when Campion sold out in 1936. It was photographed at Kent Street, Nottingham. *(Both: GHFA)*

In an agreement dated 9th June 1935, the business of Retford Coachways Limited, of Retford, was jointly taken over by East Midland Motor Services Limited and the Trent Motor Traction Company Limited. Just over a year earlier Retford had taken delivery of two AEC Regal 4s, with dual-purpose 32-seat bodywork by John Taylor Limited, of Barnsley. The Regal 4 was AEC's answer to the Leyland Lion LT series, and had a four-cylinder version of the Rackham-designed six-cylinder engine. Number **14** (**ANN 966**) *(previous page)* was one of the pair. It passed to East Midland, as did **VO 5457** *(above)*, a 1931 six-cylinder Regal, which also had Taylor 32-seat bodywork. Trent took Retford's 1932 Albion Victor DH49, **VO 7858** *(below)*. Taylor also bodied this 20-seater. All three photographs were taken at Huntingdon Street bus station, Nottingham. *(All: GHFA)*

Mention was made in the introduction of the large number of chassis makers competing for orders as the nineteen-twenties drew to a close and into the new decade. The Italian firm of Lancia was one of several foreign manufacturers offering right-hand-drive chassis for the British market. The firm achieved some success and many Lancias could be seen up to the outbreak of war in 1939. **DL 4117** *(above)*, was a Pentaiota (introduced in 1925 and the first Lancia to have front-wheel brakes) with a 20-seat canvas-roofed body of unknown make. It had been new in June 1925 to Fountain, of Cowes, Isle of Wight. Catering for the same type of business with a bonneted chassis and a body seating 20 or so passengers, Morris-Commercial was one of a number of UK operators that competed successfully against the imported makes. **CV 4852** *(below)* was a 1931 Viceroy 20-seater, new to Hawkey, of Newquay, in 1931. *(Both: OSMB/CC)*

A lot of the smaller chassis makers found the competition from Bedford, as that manufacturer got to grips with the market as the 1930s progressed, difficult to meet. Bedfords were simple, reliable, easy and cheap to maintain, and were generally without frills. Inexpensive, basic transport, in other words, and they sold in their thousands. Duple Motor Bodies, of Hendon, forged a close working relationship with Bedford, and provided bodywork for large numbers of the latter's new chassis, including **WG 4551** *(above)*, a 1936 WTB 20-seater, which had been new to Walter Alexander. By the time of this view it had been sold to Johnson's, of Henley-in-Arden. A chassis maker which ought to have done as well as the Bedford, but didn't, was Thornycroft. **UJ 5240** *(below)* was new in June 1935 as No. **12** in the Salopia, of Whitchurch, fleet. It was a Cygnet, with Shearing 32-seat coachwork of striking appearance, and was withdrawn in 1951. *(Both: OSMB/CC)*

Municipal Thirties

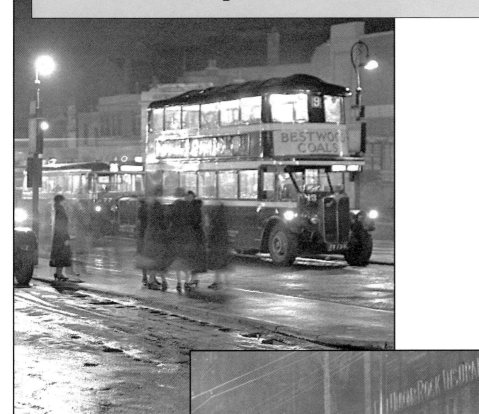

It would be hard to find a more authoritative source for illustrations of vehicles from the City of Nottingham fleet, to begin our coverage of municipalities, than the collection of Geoffrey Atkins. A resident from 1912, he has since the late 1920s covered the fleet in great detail. One of Geoffrey's happiest inspirations has been a series of after-dark shots which naturally includes some of the local municipal vehicles. AEC Regents were the mainstay in Nottingham for thirty years. These two are No. **13** (**TV 733**), dating from 1930 and bodied by English Electric, and 1936's No. **201** (**BTV 588**), which had a Metro-Cammell body. *(Both: GHFA)*

Nottingham took 40 AEC Regents in 1930: twenty bodied by English Electric, ten by Short Bros and ten by Park Royal. This beautifully composed May 1935 picture of Nottingham's Old Market includes No. **30** (**TV 1630**), the last of the Short Bros batch. *(GHFA)*

Nottingham's smaller municipal neighbour, West Bridgford Urban District Council, was also a staunch supporter of the Associated Equipment Company Limited for its vehicle purchases, buying very little else between 1926 and its demise when sold to Nottingham in 1968. Number **9** (**CRR 92**) *(above)* was one of three Park Royal-bodied 56-seaters delivered in October 1936. A highbridge bus, it was rebuilt to low-height configuration by Willowbrook in 1952 and was withdrawn in 1957. West Bridgford's No. **14** (**RR 7635**) *(below)* was an ADC 416A with Hall Lewis 32-seat dual-doorway bodywork; the rear doorway was of the "Scottish" cutaway design. The Associated Daimler Company was a temporary and unsuccessful joining of forces by AEC and Daimler in the 1920s. Number 14 was withdrawn in 1937 and served thereafter with a fairground showman. *(Both: GHFA)*

Small normal-control buses were very common in the 1930s, though perhaps less so in municipal fleets than in those of the independents. The endless quest for more seats within the dimensions allowed by the Construction & Use Regulations had already in the twenties produced designs that placed the driver alongside the engine, although the bonneted vehicle would survive into the postwar period in the shape of the Bedford OB and a few similar models. The Leyland Lioness *(above)* was also a popular choice. **WW 1881** was No. **46** in the Keighley Corporation fleet. New in 1927, with a Leyland 26-seat body, it is seen here climbing up to Thwaites Brow. It passed to the new Keighley-West Yorkshire undertaking in 1932 and was withdrawn in 1934. Bournemouth Corporation's No. **179** (**DLJ 40**) *(below)* was a Bedford WTB with Duple 25-seat bodywork. It had been new in 1937 and was lost to the War Department requisitioners in 1940. *(STA; OSMB/CC)*

<< **Previous page:** That same search for more seats brought the six-wheeled chassis into prominence at a time when longer vehicles on two axles were illegal. An imposing example of the type was Coventry's No. **56** (**VC 9665**), a Maudslay ML7 with Brush 60-seat bodywork. A 1931 machine, and perhaps a little dated in appearance, it ran for Coventry until 1939. *(STA)*

This page: Neighbouring Birmingham Corporation specified Brush 50-seat bodywork for a batch of 1929 AEC Regents. On one of Geoffrey Atkins's rare visits to that city, No. **363** (**OF 3995**) was photographed *(above)* on service 1A heading for Acocks Green, and No. **357** (**OF 3989**) *(below)* was leading three similar buses, all employed on a special service to the races. The photographs were taken in June 1930. *(Both: GHFA)*

Doncaster Corporation favoured the six-wheeled chassis with 60-seat bodywork for a time in the 1930s. A number of smaller manufacturers, such as Guy, Karrier, Maudslay and Sunbeam, offered such chassis, but Leyland and AEC gave them stiff competition respectively with the Titanic and Renown. Leyland's inaptly named Titanic did not sell in huge numbers, but AEC achieved respectable sales of the Renown, mainly through the 1,439 examples in the London Transport fleet. Doncaster ran both side-by-side. Number **66** (**DT 5337**) entered the fleet in August 1934 as the first of five Renowns and ran until July 1949 *(above)*. It had bodywork by Charles H Roe, as did Leyland Titanic Gearless TT3c No. **72** (**DT 7812**) *(below)*, new in 1936 and one of nine Titanics in the Doncaster fleet. It had torque-converter transmission when new, was fitted with a conventional clutch and gearbox in 1946, and was withdrawn in 1949. *(GHFA Collection; GHFA)*

Above: Rotherham Corporation was a convert to the Bristol B when that full-sized chassis appeared, taking 13 between August 1928 and December 1929. All but one (bodied by the operator) had Roe bodies, and all were centre-entrance 32-seaters. This example is thought to be one of Roe-bodied Nos **104-6 (EF 5858-60)**, delivered in September 1929.

Below: Rotherham attracted much attention in 1934/5 by placing in service a batch of 11 single-ended double-deck tramcars - an unusual layout for the British Isles. Number **2** was new in April 1935. It was fitted with English Electric 63-seat bodywork, EMB hornless bogies and two GEC 40hp motors. It had fixed bus-type seats facing forwards and the contrast in external appearance when compared to the traditional Sheffield tram behind could hardly be more marked. Number 2 was withdrawn in 1949. *(Both: GHFA)*

Above: The forward-control single-decker, usually of half-cab design and - since the mid 1920s - mounted on a pneumatic-tyred chassis, was versatile, being adaptable for everything from the most lavishly equipped private hire coaches to the humble service bus. The four-cylinder-engined Leyland Lion took a goodly share of the market for such vehicles, the PLSC versions of the mid 1920s developing into the LT range which flourished throughout the following decade. Lincoln Corporation's No. **4 (VL 1262)** was an LT1 with 32-seat bodywork by Bracebridge. It ran for Lincoln for 20 years, from 1929 to 1949. It was photographed in Skegness.

Below: Lincoln's Leyland Titan TD1 No. **32 (VL 848)** was a Leyland bodied open-staircase 48-seater. New in 1928, it also lasted until 1949. The picture was taken circa 1933 in St Mary Street, Lincoln. *(Both: GHFA)*

Above: Lincoln Corporation's preference for Leylands saw an intake of TD5 Titans with Leyland highbridge bodywork in 1937/8. Number **48** (**AFE 84**), a 56-seater, was new in October 1937 and lasted until 1955 when Lincoln withdrew it and later sold it for scrap. It is seen here at the terminus in Monks Road, Lincoln, in 1938.

Below: Lincoln's No. **58** (**AFE 375**) was an April 1938 arrival. It also had Leyland bodywork, this time seating 55. It was withdrawn in 1954 and found further use until 1958 with the independent operator Hornsby, who traded as Primrose Coaches, of Ashby. After withdrawal by Hornsby the bus was scrapped. The photograph was taken in 1938 as the bus passed over Lincoln's Central Station level crossing *(Both: GHFA)*

Above: The Guy bus chassis was by no means unknown before the war, but it was the vast numbers of wartime utility Arabs, which in turn led to a healthy postwar order book, that set the Wolverhampton-based manufacturer on the map as a provider of chassis for public service vehicle use. Earlier examples had included some six-wheelers, including Derby Corporation's No. **28 (CH 8829),** one of three FCX66 models delivered in 1929. Number 28 had a 65-seat body by Ransomes and ran for Derby until 1945.

Below: An earlier 1929 entry into Derby's fleet had been No. **22 (CH 8340),** which was an Associated Daimler Type 422 chassis carrying 48-seat bodywork by the Loughborough coachbuilder Brush. The vehicle lasted a decade in Derby service and there is no known trace of it after its 1939 withdrawal. *(Both: GHFA)*

Above: In 1930 Derby Corporation took delivery of fleet number **35** (**CH 9503**), a two-axled Guy FC48 chassis fitted with a Brush Coachworks 48-seat body. After withdrawal in 1942 it was acquired by Wiggs & Sons Limited, trading as Grey Coaches, of London SE15. The photograph was taken in Corporation Street, Derby, in June 1930.

Below: The Derby fleet was varied and of great interest. This 1928 single-decker was an AEC 427 with a 28-seat rear-entrance body by Sanderson & Holmes. Number **13** (**CH 7881**) lasted until 1934 - a short life even by the standards of the nineteen-thirties. It was photographed in Midland Road, Derby.

>> *Opposite page:* An early example of the Bristol B-type chassis was No. **40** (**RA 1809**) in the Chesterfield Corporation fleet. The 32-seat centre-entrance bodywork was by Reeve & Kenning. This scene at Vicar Lane, Chesterfield, was taken in March 1934. *(All: GHFA)*

Above: The Chesterfield Corporation fleet only ever had one Leyland TS4 Tiger. Number **49** (**RB 7830**) was new in February 1933 and ran until 1947 and then for an independent until 1951. The dual-doorway body seating 34 was by Leyland. This was an early example of a Gearless Tiger with torque-converter transmission; the photographer recalls how, at the time of this March 1934 photograph, the vehicle's driver demonstrated the workings of the transmission system to him.

Below: Chesterfield's No. **68** (**RB 9313**) was a later Gearless Tiger, of type TS6c, new in December 1933 and withdrawn in 1946. This time the bodywork was by Metro-Cammell and had 32-seats. The picture was taken in Chesterfield in March 1935. *(Both: GHFA)*

Above: Another of Chesterfield's Metro-Cammell-bodied TS6c Tigers, No. **70** (**RB 9315**), was caught on the move in Beetwell Street, Chesterfield, passing a wonderfully evocative radio shop. The wireless was then perhaps past its infancy, but was still - and would remain until the advent of television - an enormously popular pastime. This is another March 1935 picture.

Below: Contemporary with the Metro-Cammell TS6c single-decker in Chesterfield was the Titan TD3 double-decker. This one, No. **73** (**RB 9308**), a lowbridge 48-seater from the same bodybuilder, was new in December 1933 and lasted until 1945 when it was sold for scrap. This view, also in Chesterfield, was taken in July 1935. *(Both: GHFA)*

Above: The Leyland Titan TD3 with Meto-Cammell bodywork was also a feature of the Manchester Corporation fleet in the mid 1930s. This one was No. **530** (**AXJ 861**), a 54-seater, seen at Manchester Piccadilly in May 1935, two months after it had entered service. This vehicle ran for 16 years, being withdrawn and sold for scrap in 1951. The landmark Lewis's sign would not last until the turn of the Century.

Below: In the same month at the same place, but facing the opposite way, the photographer caught a bustling scene in which Manchester Corporation and North Western vehicles act as backcloth for Oldham Corporation's No. **19** (**BU 8255**), which was a 1934 Leyland Tiger TS6 with 32-seat fully fronted bodywork by Charles H Roe, of Leeds. Oldham withdrew the vehicle in 1949. Wartime redevelopment by the Luftwaffe changed the skyline to that seen today. *(Both: GHFA)*

A contemporary double-decker in the Oldham fleet was No. **58 (BU 7946)**, a 1934 Titan TD3 with English Electric 54-seat highbridge bodywork. Withdrawn in 1948, it was rebodied as a 33-seat coach by Bellhouse & Hartwell and sold to Dimbleby, of Ashover, who ran it until 1960. *(STA/BCVM)*

Above: Leyland and AEC had to fight hard for their supremacy in the nineteen-thirties market place. Daimler perhaps provided the toughest competition and their products were seen in fleets all over the British Isles. **ANM 834** was No. **53** in the Luton Corporation fleet. New in 1936, it was an oil-engined COG5 model with Willowbrook 52-seat lowbridge bodywork. It was withdrawn in 1954 and sold for scrap.

Below: An earlier Daimler, on a CP6 petrol-engined chassis, **FW 3762** was No. **9** in the fleet of Cleethorpes Urban District Council. New in April 1933, it was scrapped in 1952. The bodywork, again by Willowbrook, was to 52-seat highbridge specification. *(Both: STA)*

Thirties Trolleybuses

Trolleybuses were a feature of the nineteen-thirties as they were of perhaps no other decade. Just as those ten years witnessed the waning of the tram in Great Britain, so it saw the trolleybus wax as it never would again. Nottingham had been an enthusiastic user since 1927 when, in 1931, twenty-five 60-seaters were ordered from Karrier and Ransomes, with the bodywork orders going respectively to Park Royal and Brush. This scene on a misty September 1935 day at Nottingham's Victoria station has pedestrians skipping nimbly out of the path of No. **39** (**TV 4477**), one of the Ransomes/Brush machines. The photograph shows the wide spacing of the trolleybus wires, which were later brought closer together. *(GHFA)*

Above: Derby Corporation's Guy BTX trolleybus No. **83** (**RC 405**) had a Brush body with, despite the three-axled chassis, only 56 seats. The vehicle was fitted with a Rees Roturbo 75hp motor and had been new in January 1932. It was photographed in July 1932 at Market Place, Derby. Trolleybuses had less chance of further service when sold by their first owner than did motor buses, although such use was not unknown. This one had no such good fortune and was withdrawn in 1949 and scrapped.

Below: Number **161** (**RC 6661**) in the Derby fleet was a Daimler CTM4 with Brush 54-seat bodywork. It was placed in service in November 1938 and withdrawn in 1959 after an accident, as a consequence of which it was scrapped. The photograph dates from 1939 and was taken at Derby LMS station. *(Both: GHFA)*

Above: The neighbouring municipality of Chesterfield was also a trolleybus user. Its system was inaugurated in May 1927 but did not last out the following decade, being abandoned on 24th March 1938. Number **14** (**RA 1823**) had been new in July 1927. It was a Straker-Clough with Reeve & Kenning centre-entrance 32-seat bodywork and BTH 60hp motor. On closure of the system in 1938 it was scrapped. It was at Stephenson Place, Chesterfield, in March 1934. Note the unusual "one-over-the-other" arrangement of the trolley booms.

Below: Another March 1934 shot illustrates Chesterfield's double-decker No. **16** (**RB 4890**), a 1931 Ransomes D2 with lowbridge 48-seat bodywork by the same manufacturer. It was one of a pair (Nos 16/7), one of which (identity unknown) was exhibited at the 1931 Commercial Motor Show. Despite being only seven years old, this one (as was the entire trolleybus fleet) was also scrapped when the system closed. *(Both; GHFA)*

Above: Even earlier into trolleybus operation was Birmingham, who ordered 12 Roe-bodied 51-seat Railless machines in 1922. Fleet numbers 1-12 (OK 4823-34) were archaic in appearance with a good deal of the tramcar about them: indeed they were driven by means of a tramcar-type controller. They had Dick Kerr electrical equipment and two English Electric 42hp motors. All were withdrawn in 1932. It is not known which one of the 12 features in this photograph.

Below: By 1926 Birmingham's new trolleybuses were visually still remarkably old fashioned. Number **17** (**ON 3261**) was the first in the fleet to be fitted with a foot-operated controller. It was a Vickers-bodied 52-seat AEC, which was also withdrawn in 1932. A May 1930 photograph. *(Both: GHFA)*

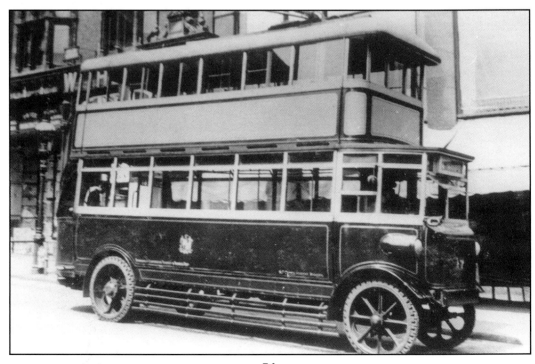

Above: As the thirties moved along Birmingham's conservative ideas on body styling ensured that their vehicles continued to look older than they were, a trend that was to mark the fleet until well into the postwar period. Trolleybus No. **16** (**OJ 1016**), a 1932 AEC 663T with Short Bros 58-seat body, replaced one of the solid-tyred withdrawals of that year. Withdrawn in 1940, No. 16 was stored during the war years and then sold for scrap in 1945. *(OSMB/CC)*

Below: A large batch of Leyland TTBD2s with MCCW 58-seat bodies (Nos 17-66) was bought for the Birmingham fleet in 1934, typified by No. **35** (**OC 1135**), seen here on a gloomy, wet day soon after entering service. It was withdrawn and scrapped in 1951. *(STA)*

Above: Smartly dressed familes with children descend from Doncaster Corporation No. **18** (**DT 2003**) on a dull summer Sunday in 1930. The trolleybus was almost new, having entered service in January of that year. It was a 61-seat Roe-bodied Karrier E6, which would last in Doncaster service only until July 1938.

Below: Even worse weather in September 1936 for this view of Bradford Corporation's AEC 661T No. **630** (**AAK 432**). Fitted with English Electric 80hp motor and 58-seat bodywork, it was new in October 1935, rebodied by Northern Coachbuilders in August 1947, withdrawn in 1958 and sold for scrap in July 1960. *(Both: GHFA)*

Company Thirties

Operators affiliated to the big groups - Tilling or BET - were responsible for a certain amount of conformity in body styling through the purchasing power of their central buying authorities and thus identical, or very similar, vehicles could be seen in widely separated areas. Many such bulk orders from the British Electrical Federation (on behalf of the BET companies) went to Brush Coachworks, of Loughborough. Thames Valley's No. **239** (**RX 9307**) had a 28-seat Brush body for use on the Reading to London express service. *(STA/BCVM)*

Above: Southdown Motor Services Limited found a need for bonneted vehicles rather later into the 1930s than did most other operators. **CUF 319** was a Leyland RLTB3 Tigress - a most unusual breed - dating from July 1936. Originally carrying fleet number 319, it was renumbered **1819** in about 1938. The 20-seat centre-entrance bodywork with folding roof was by Burlingham. It was withdrawn in 1952. This photograph was at Portslade Works. *(Denis Clark Collection/Eric Surfleet)*

Below: Earlier Leyland bonneted models had included this example of the Lioness, which with its six-cylinder engine was really a normal-control Tiger rather than Lion. Southdown's No. 316 (**UF 8830**) was a 1933 LTB1 with 20-seat rear-entrance coachwork by Thomas Harrington, of Hove. Originally canvas roofed, it was modernised and fitted with glass quarter lights circa 1938 and renumbered **1816**. *(OSMB/CC)*

Above: Another substantial rebuilding job was done on Wilts & Dorset's Leyland TS1 Tiger No. **85** (**MW 6293**). New in June 1930 with Heaver 30-seat dual-doorway coachwork, its original canvas roof was removed in March 1933 and replaced with a panelled roof and luggage container; the forward door was also removed. Then in 1938, as shown in the picture, the chassis was rebodied by Harrington as a 32-seater with entrance at the rear. After further rebuilding by the operator in 1945 it was withdrawn and sold in 1953.

Below: Wilts & Dorset No. **166** (**BWV 663**) was a 1939 lowbridge Leyland Titan TD5, bodied by Park Royal as a 52-seater. It was found to be in need of rebuilding in 1948, and the work was done by Portsmouth Aviation. The vehicle was withdrawn in 1956. *(Both: OSMB/CC)*

<< *Opposite page:* Gargantuan private hire jobs were a feature of the prewar years. In this October 1935 scene Walter Alexander's No. **263** (**WG 3487**), a 1935 Leyland Tiger TS7 bodied as a 32-seat front-entrance coach by the operator, heads a fleet of at least 11 more vehicles on an assignment for the Chester Unionist Association. **P236/9** (**WG 3469/72**) can also be identified. All three were rebuilt to TD4 specification and rebodied as double-deckers in 1943.

Above: Western Welsh, in June of the same year, needed at least 28 vehicles to convey delegates to the Co-operative Wholesale Society conference in Cardiff. The leading vehicle, and the only one positively identifiable, was No. **59** (**UH 8213**), a 1930 Leyland Lion LT2 with Northern Counties 32-seat bus body. *(Both: STA/BCVM)*

Above: Bus services had to be kept going, regardless of conditions, and here a brand new Ribble Leyland Titan TD1, No. **1071** (**CK 4428**), fitted with Leyland 48-seat lowbridge bodywork, negotiates a flooded Lancashire country road on its way into Burnley in June 1931. The conductor leans out of the bus, perhaps wondering whether the water will rise above platform level.

Below: West Yorkshire's No. **419** (**WW 8363**), a 1929 Titan TD1 with open-staircase 51-seat Leyland bodywork, was having to deal with slush on the roads during a March 1931 snowfall. The road surface suggests water rather than ice, so the uphill journey out to Silsden was perhaps not too hazardous, though the upper-deck passengers would have seen little through the front windows. *(Both: STA/BCVM)*

Above: Sheffield United Tours, then only recently under the joint ownership of East Midland, North Western and Yorkshire Traction, put this AEC Regal II into service in June 1937. **DWA 993** was fleet number **S.104**, and had Burlingham 32-seat coachwork. It was in its first month of service in this view on Scarborough's Marine Drive. It was withdrawn in 1950, by then carrying a different body from an identical vehicle. *(GHFA)*

Below: The North Western Road Car Company Limited put this Tiger TS1 into service in 1931. Number **514** **(DB 9414)** when new had a Harrington 26-seat rear entrance coach body. This picture shows it as rebodied, also by Harrington, in 1934 as a front-entrance 32-seater. North Western's penchant for body swapping would continue for another 20 years or so. DB 9414 was withdrawn in 1947 but survived into the 1950s working for a travelling fairground showman. *(STA)*

Above: Rather basic transport for a private hire job to the seaside. Eastern Counties No. **A192** (**NG 2727**), a 1932 Leyland Titan TD2 with operator-built lowbridge bodywork, had taken a party to Skegness in July 1934. The vehicle was rebodied as a highbridge 56-seater by Eastern Coach Works (the Eastern Counties Coach Factory renamed in 1936) in 1940 and renumbered AH192. It was withdrawn and sold for scrap in 1950.

Below: An Eastern Counties single-decker on its way from East Anglia to Liverpool had called in at Huntingdon Street bus station, Nottingham, in this July 1937 scene. The vehicle was **LJ3** (**NG 9903**), a 1935 Bristol JJW with Eastern Counties 32-seat coachwork. It was withdrawn and sold for scrap in 1957, its longevity in the fleet having been aided by a body rebuild, done by Watson, of Lowestoft, in April 1947. *(Both: GHFA)*